Forth into Light

Poems
and
Pictures of Faith

By

George Reynolds, O.P.

NEW PRIORY PRESS
EXPLORING THE DOMINICAN VISION

ii

In Church, we should all be wearing crash helmets;
ushers should issue life preservers and signal flares;
they should lash us to our pews. For the sleeping god
may wake someday and take offense, or the waking
god may draw us out to where we can never return.

Annie Dillard
An Expedition to the Pole

INTRODUCTION

We all live, I believe, in world of contradictions, contrasts and confusion. The only way we reconcile that world within us with the world around us is through faith and love. "If you had the faith the size of a mustard seed..." "And the greatest of these is love."

By faith we believe in ourselves and see in the universe the incredible creation of a loving God. And with love, we embrace it.

Anyone who has ever been amazed at a sunset and stands in awe and silence is a poet; just as anyone who has reflected on life within with honesty, realizes we all have a novel, a novella or a short story within us. We need to appreciate the great gift given to us and for us; and it is speaking to us in the silence of our hearts.

There comes a magic moment in our lives that make the contradictions into a candle in the midnight darkness; the contraries into a unity; the confusions into a moment of peace and grace.

"And He saw the world He had made and pronounced it good."

May the goodness of the world burst forth in the goodness of our lives so we may share our goodness with the goodness of God and of others. And that is the virtue of hope.

Fr. George Reynolds, OP
St, Pius Priory,
Chicago, Illinois

Table of Contents

Forth into Light

Poems and
Pictures of Faith

2

CREATION

Once upon a time ago,
Many ages as the world is young,
When darkness shone in the blind-black day,
God thought and said and in thinking made,
Let there be light.
Light gleamed and bled and gashed:
One day.
Into the light walked stars and moons,
Light lanterns hung in mirthful play
Like great cast dice.
And God said,
Let there be
To the hills and waves
To the valleys floored in springtime reds
Against a veil of hope's pure greens.
And birds swam while fishes flew
In mingled ecstasy
To settle in their proper spheres of praise.
New notes were heard through drenching starshine
      and ocean breaks,
Over the thunder-rich applause of a billion songs of good,
Let there be,
Said God, liking his litany,
Let there be an allegro to life. Let there be love!
Dawn blasted its dappled light as love laughed.
The echo of Love sparkled in the rush of winds.
Pauperwise, immensely rich, the naked millionaire,
Surveyed his realm and laughed and found it wanting.
He whispered to the carrion bird that fed his soul,
Let there be!
And death was born.
And with it came the violence of summer floods
That pick just-dropped autumn leaves
And stored them in alcoved eddies of too-late knowledge.

On vulture's vans the flapping sounds of curses
    pierced the night.
And in this tightness of subzero steps on crunching snow,
Above the cynic's screech, above the howl of jackal's prey,
Was heard the distant echo of victorious defeat:
I am!
You are not.
I am not yet through with my creation.
Let there be hope.
When you are old, says God, you will know
    the meaning of my youth.
I will raise man to a parable which is itself
    a parable to man.
I will give you fear discernible only in a splintered joy.
And I will give you and teach you Generosity,
Uncommanded self's self in pyres
To burn in watchfulness for your ship-wrecked soul.
And, one day, in hope,
You will be reconciled,
Not as a soldier who makes his sick peace
With the bullets across his breast,
But as the stars
That clang their portals shut
On the sight of too much happiness.

PASSION

Introduction:

For everything there is a season
    And a time for every occupation under heaven.
A time for birth
    And a time for death.
A time for betrayal
    And a time for redemption.
A time for darkness
    And a time for light.
A time for faith
    And a time to question that faith.
A time for pain
    And a time for joy.
A time for solitude
    And a time for sharing.
But now is the time for the powers   of darkness,
    The hour of betrayal and pain.
A time for fears and tears
And the moment of the love-cursed kiss.

PILLOW TALK

Come; lay your drowsy head upon my willing breast;
Hold me in your warmth with truth
And sing with me the death of moons.
For we have matters of great moment,
Things too weighty for the sun to hear
And must sacramentalize the Now of Choice.
I reel at invading visions and unselected sounds
That clamor in my love

    Do walruses have to shave at five,
    Or jumbo jets feel pain in flight?
    Do fish lack lids, better to see the piercing sun,
    And do trumpets announce more victories than defeats?
    If Twain could sing, would cellos beat a faster fugue
    Or would he find an oboe more at ease?
    Does blood become the mountain's life at dusk
    And do night spirits ride upon Sandia's crest?
    Does Bach still play his tunes for faded royalty
    And Purcell herald Queen Anne's death?
    Does green become your youth that haunts the corridors
    Of thought?
    And can you turn to lavender at Will?
    Have you prayed your dreams to birth,
    And midwived the secrets or your heart?

I hear your voice in all the words I use,
Your accents are the truth of life.
Do not leave the hollow of my arms to wander
    in the shoreless sea,
But take my wings
And watch the serpent, far below, give shelter
    to the eagle's fears.

CHRIST SPEAKS

It is not death I taste in this bleak hour
As much as beauty that will not be seen.
Here, crippled by my Father's love,
As much as beauty that will not be seen
I stand and wait for some dark friend
Who'd breathe fresh hope into my failing heart?
But callow curses call me back to pain.
Both friend and hope have died unborn, unknown.
Around my head the sound of surf is heard.
Engulfed in sound and surf I wake to drown
In cascading night and puny power.
All hands are air around my unlit pyre.
And even blackness is my welcomed home.

THE TEARS OF PETER

Too late for tears
    Too soon for contrition,
We stand on the emptiness of triple lies,
  Thrice told,
  And weep.
The lifetime of invested love
  Lies shattered in one dark night
And ashes surround the building of my ruins.
The rag-ends of all my days
Are gathered into one deep look
That comes from sleepless eyes.
And all the tears
  Of all the blind lions
Are united in my loss.

JUDAS SPEAKS:

Before the river ran with Pharaoh's blood
Or fishes swam in hidden ocean depths;
Before the mountains captured cloud-tossed snow
Or even a rainbow pledged a covenant of peace,
This moment was foreseen, foreknown, and willed.
It had to come, and I the one to bring it.
Inevitable as the lifting mist, heralding another dawn,
Inexorable as the floods of spring that portend
    a graceful crop,
The battle and the field were drawn
By an ineluctable thread, a web,
Which grew around the majesty of double defeat.
It is a fearful thing to be an instrument of fate
And know the prophet is a leprous guest.
What I have done, I have done for you.
Do you not feel the tingle of the kiss upon your lips
Or shiver in this garden night?

So now the truth is out, completely out and bare,
And supple flesh is heir to kingdoms of its choice.
The two of us upon our trees will hang;
Both of us shall pierce the angry sky;
Like misshapen twins our deaths are chained
But his wounds will heal in peals of time-chocked praise
And, overhead, the title king is his.
But as for me—
For me, a casual youth, searching for a sickly lamb,
Will indifferently look up and say,
"There is Judas hanging,
He lost his way."

UNANSWERED QUESTIONS

Oh, my people.
What have I done to you?
How have I offended you?
Answer me.

Before me danced the new-born stag
    and rills of melting snow.
With gentle, tender thought I gave you
    springtime's praise and winter's rest.
For this my sight is blinded with my pain
And blood blurs my eyes.

Oh, my people.

I gave you caressing Eastern winds
    that suck fresh life from barren crags;
I gave you healing rains and leaping greens.
For this I number all the blows
    your jealousy calls forth.

For a crown my Father gave me stars
and you have crowned my head with thorns.
To your lame, I gave the gift of speed;
To your blind, I gave the gift of sight;
To your deaf, I gave the gift of sound.
And you have given me the burden of your thoughtlessness.
For dignity, humiliation;
For sunrise, hate;
And for life—
for life you have given me another's tomb.

Oh, my people.
What have I done to you?

I gave you vines of bursting grapes
to fill your mirth with honest song.
For this you laugh at my swollen hands and battered mouth.
I gave you fields of golden wheat
to feed your young and ease your age.
For this you give me mockery for food and gall to drink.

Oh, my people.
What have I done to you?
How have I offended you?

Is it because I gave you life
that you demand my death?
That I gave you living waters
in the parched desert of your hate,
Or that my truth is stronger than your lies,
And my gifts more beautiful
than your sullen crafts,
That now I wear a blood-dried robe
and hold a jester's rod?

I would have carried you upon my shoulders
As a shepherd his favorite lamb.

Oh, my people.
What have I done to you?
How have I offended you?
    Answer me.

EASTER

The numbered days, unnumbered run,
And Christ lies slain in the ruins of our hate.
For life, no answer comes from unasked questions
Nor are questions lost on unformulated phrase.
For death, bells toll the April of our hope.
The Cross, the Crown, transformed by blood and dust
While Spirit takes dissembled bones and breathes fresh life,
Demanding that the soul stand tall.
The empty tomb, devoid of flesh, sends light
Into the shadows of our doubt.
It sings of shredded shrouds and the defeated worm.
The granite, devoid of purpose, proclaims a promise kept.
And the laughing sentinel keeps watch over air and grace;
It tells the women that their tears are vain.
The knell of death, transformed into a victory cry,
Rings silently on weekday's birth
While pregnant hills give up their guests to sunrise rays.
The birthday of the sun is here,
Celebrated in the morning mist.

Our hope has roots, though growing
    with the brambles' curse,
And the temerity of flight blushes at its adolescent fears.
The tomb, the guard, the loved, proclaim a message,
    awesome and alive,
That on Easter morning, Death died.

THE VIETNAM PEASANT

If you would let me be a man,
Do not take from me my right to pain,
Your fingers clutch at phantoms
When you grasp for puppets string.
If we must sit in jungle trees
And listen to the song of blood,
We hold our adolescence, unfettered by public rites,
A thing too dear to hold.
Stardust is too cheap in graves.
My buffalo, my god;
My gun, my hoe;
My plot, my world.
Why sit in doomed swamps and merely dream my sleep?
To be a man, I must be free,
With green and white wings
To fly over grey froth and purple hills.
Let my rainbow be the layers of sadness.
Let me feel muscular power, surge in supple limbs.
Let me stride my land and feel contempt
    for the unborn grain,
Distance from the waiting worm.
Let etched stone proclaim my youth
And let those I have killed smile and say,
"Only in the peasant is found beauty."

THE ANGRY CLOWN

Tenseness grows as the ring goes dark
And the sudden light startles expectant faces.
He appears in gold,
Like a god, judgment and reward on either side.
His bloodless face transforms the tent
And laughter waits for cause to burst.
His baggy pants fall down
While his water-walking shoes clap the dirt.
The apple nose with its elastic band crumbles
    to the cheek
And the ears-wide mouth moves in so undless shock.
It is not enough.
We have seen too many clowns at finer times
    to abandon moderation.
A frenzy of pie pans and prat falls cannot unclog the hush.
And so the eyes, encased in paint and grease, find their
    haven in contempt.
On every face the paint and grease,
In every ear the silence of fear.
It is not the folly of the harlequin we applaud

But he who sees our folly, distanced by our doubt.
We cannot laugh at foibles we do not own
Or spook at demons laid to rest.
Parading elephants and dancing bears cannot interrupt
    the tension of despair.
Nor masks of joy make hollow sounds replete.
The clown cannot capture an alien love
And we cannot thump our hands at magic
    that doubts itself.

FAITH AND THE SHELL

The sympathetic surge of waves,
Their unheard each imprisoned in the fragile shell,
Belie by size their meaning and their grace
To mock the continents they join.
Aborted by sheer intensity,
The single wave that carries silent gulls
Sends forth a symphony of peace
And drowns the starfish in its quest for caves.
All the while, the conch rests lightly on the palm,
Containing all the sound and all the hope
That all the voyagers forgot.
The haunting strain is heart beyond the heart,
The notes a unity with salt-spume light
Reflected in a diamond eye,
Like lover whales returning to their winter home.
This minor universe rejects the lesser soul;
It sings for one and one alone its tear-specked song
Now orchestrated by the rhythmic pulse of pain.
But once that melody is ever heard

All other sounds are merely noise,
And mermaids laugh, unnoticed, just in sight of land.

FAITH AND THE SHELL #2

The crippling sands lie empty in their promise.
Golden in their light, they suck the life from stars
And shift their messages into patterned rills.
Derisive sounds they make against a never-winter wind.
But settled in their dunes, the vast enigma grows
And brazens out the lies, and waits.
It waits for birth—its own—from the blistered sun
To die reborn and beautiful.
The grace within the shell bursts forth
And its nucleus of splintered dreams weeps joy.
Juxtaposed against its nightless moon and dayless skies
Its vastness beats a robe of hope.
It thrills the blood in bloodless veins and bleaches leprous
     bones.
Enigma still, enigmatic to itself, it shames the sands with
     truth.
Ten thousand thousand cries of peace, released amid the
     crystal cries,
Revive and live.
And each felt grain becomes itself,
     Golden in its light;
          Golden in its love.

FAITH AND THE PATH

The second end is comfort after bitter ways and plans.
Preludes to introductions to overtures are costly
To the twice twisted heart.
The cursed prophesy of sweat and pain
Is fulfilled in the guests of exile.
For no castle moves before the king in flight
And no cloud hides chambers with blazing hearths.
Each journey tokens ruins left behind
And unbuilt homes ahead,
With the accompaniment of shock and doubt
Like a forgotten shadow that will not move or stay.
If kings find solace in the taunts of fools
And fools find wisdom in the folly of their kings,
Then there is more than hope and less than life
In the journey's end.
But how to know the end as end
Or as some brief stop, a respite from the wandering moon
And decaying light?
Those who wear prophetic robes consider first their jug
And withered palms;
But they do not mock the Voice by sleep
Or the Word by silence
Nor the act by death.
A journey seeks or flees by faith
And not by thought;
Every path is carved by its own star
And tended by its own Rose.

FAITH AND DOUBT

The fear that gnaws my guts is not the fear of pain
But the fear of numbness.
The fear that rules my thoughts is not the fear of death
But the fear of being ignored by life.
The terror that grips my heart and stifles my breath
Is not the fear of destroying relationships
But of having no relationships to destroy.
The dread that dominates my waking hours and invades
    my fitful sleep is the dread,
Not of forgetfulness,
But of having nothing to remember.
The fear of love is stronger than the fear of hate,
And the fear of both pervades my listless hope.
The fear of rejection is more threatening
    than the promise of fulfilled risks.
The fear of friendship is not less strong
    than the fear of loneliness.

But it is only through fear that greatness is measured;
For more deadly battles have been won in the conflicts
    of the heart
Than on the bloody fields of war.

FAITH AND THE STATUE

If the statue weeps, will it ever be the same?
Or is there some sometime when the tears are pearls,
Fresh-hatched from silent, secret oyster wounds?
Regard the statue, clear-crafted in its garden nest,
Shrouded by its startime mist.
The roses, too, are hidden from the light
But majestically they bow to bidding winds.
The whorl of fog leaves upon the statue's cheeks
Its impress, distillation of the night.
And the garden(now)lies pregnant with the dawn
That spawns a laughing sun.
And in that birth the pearls are irrelevant to the Rose.
The mother-wisdom of the stone smiles lightly,
Rejecting to turn traitor to its marble dreams,
Calls forth the warmth of love, reflected twice,
And, in her radiance, she sleeps.

FAITH AND AGE

The full-fleshed phantoms of my night
Return to haunt the day-light facts of all my dreams.
From them I suck the lure of life
And grow with giant's vans.
Not air but clouds I beat,
And the ascendance is real.
Touched hands still touch, still are warm,
Still are felt, beyond the velvet sheath of time.
The emanating scents of scenes are here,
One more loved ghost that cradles my breath,
Giving warmth and peace before the blackened embers
    of my youth.
Many, so many faces crowd my joy,
Demand and receive my homage, shared speech
    through love.
From them I feel the eyes of Tiresias look out
And hear raged Philomel transformed,
While I lie comfortably woven in my tapestry of time.

FAITH AND THE KINGDOM

Who is King of star-swept skies,
Or lordly prince of forest's greens?
Who breathes soul into fennel's charm
And brews mandrake in a witch's fire?
Perhaps the dreamer and the fool are one
To relinquish reign for a jungle's lure.
The kingdom of the heart distends
And grows beyond the magic of the spell that burns,
Joining ice to ice.
Vine-choked-trees may be the symbol
    that the quest is done.
For what once was is still,
Like granite in the river bed,
Which grows unearthed, sublime, in the summer sun.

FAITH AND BATTLE

When the stench of battle leaves the ashes to their fate
And the clouds of waste have settled in the hills,
Then we shall know the lost as lost
And count ourselves among the uncounted dead.
The conflict, no longer desperate, forms its own rest;
That rest is fraught with shadows of despair.
What weapons lay in arsenals of dust;
What diplomatic tongue, tied to silence, clucks like crows
    in winter's nights?
Wishes jumble in rusted armor,
While corroded dreams shrivel in the fear of light.
Once more "to me" rings hollow;
No one rises to bloodied brace of threats
And we cannot tell who won this day.
But was there victory or defeat?
Of what, for whom?
Valiant efforts are no less valiant
Nor second efforts lost in thought.
Somehow, I think, the ashes laugh in the whirlwind
    of the quick;
They see beneath the stumps to next season's growth
And feel the worm move gently at their feet.

FAITH AND MAGIC

I have seen too many gorgons
To doubt the monster's breath;
Have felt too many sudden chills
To question the mountain's height;
I have heard too many melodies
To shut out unexpected airs;
Have trembled at too many shadows
To ignore the substance of despair.
All felt thrills are preparations
For unprepared-for grace.
And the intensity for life
Makes life itself intense.
A journey without pain
Can be the greatest pain of all.
Two years are too many for rest,
Too few for peace,
As each day lives in its own horizon.
The zenith of the sun is not in this galaxy of stars

But in the heart's deeper cave.
For the magic is at magic works
If the magician is not too cautious of his wares.

FAITH AND THE PEARLS

But pearls are white, the people cried,
And that's as it should be.
For white reflects, gives back the light,
Remaining pure, untouched, except by sight.
Ah, no! the dreamer thought.
Beauty is found in the oyster's pain;
By taking to itself the needs and dreams of ocean depths,
The pearl becomes the darkness.
It retains within itself its lustrous light
And bears half-whispered hopes
Made only to the fleeing moon.
It shows a thirst for growth beyond its oyster world.
The white is nice and much admired
On a lover's breast.
But the mystery of the dark is lovelier,
More dangerous,
More filled with grace.

FAITH AND THE HERON

A bird flies out and with it go our dreams,
Winged song sung in silence.
The heron cry of freedom's flight
Too shrill for human ears, merely, to hear,
Reproaches coming night with mockery.

Eluding the lure of sheltered pines
Or rocked enclaves,
The flight sweeps on beyond the forest's protecting rim
Or the beach's naked stretch or the surf's soft kiss.

Alone and yet not lonely,
suspended in the twilight of the thought and fact,
Of the desire and peace,
Of the chaos and charm,
A trilled note no monarch could distain
Makes fertile the hope, too strong a promise to ignore,
That rock and wave and pine
Work their magic on the heron's heart.

The wings stretch out and skud updrafting themes
To seek Orion, forever frozen in his forever quest,
Beautiful and bold,
Stolid and invincible,
Resplendent in his shocking light.

FAITH AND THE OWL

Before the owl grew feathers for his nights
Or winded arches dwindled in the sun,
The light from one small star began its journey to the sea
And for one brief span
Reflect its brilliance toward the sands.
But within that unmatched moment, written on
    the starshine life,
Was the history of creation's call
And the mystery of the journey's end.
For the lost youth of an aging hubris shed no tears.
But send beyond the moon the meaning missed
And laugh the orphan dawn to birth.
The owl curls up his feathers for the day,
And the winded arches stand silent in the sun.

FAITH AND AGE #2

Corridors are long when doors are shut;
Days less noble when marked by clouds.
Time more slow when set by clocks
And laughter less full when beckoned by anecdotes.
In felt absence rests the promise,
Linking memory to wish, light to shadow,
Obviating ritual by fulfillment.
Voyages are noted for their return;
Energies for their effect.
Youth and age are yoked in each by each,
Over-shadowing the darkness of what is gone.
United dreams burn more true than touched hands.
For memory holds more than what has been
And delays are mere preludes to completed peace.

FAITH AND THE CLOCK

They say that clocks tell time
And beat their lives through constant sounds
    and pleasing shapes.
But clocks and cowards lie, you know.
Both misread time through hands that do not feel,
Through faces that do not shine.
For all their clever gears and well-wrought springs,
    they lie.
The brassy tocks of clocks cannot count
Nor can little sticks tell us what is real.
Their paltry truths pass on
And their speech is one-way chance.
It is unshared communication—and lies!
Hands must touch, not point;
Faces must laugh, not glare.
And the only real beating is the sound of hearts,
Themselves constant and in tune
With the cosmic rhythm of love.

FAITH AND THE HUNGRY STARS

Within the turmoil of the shell a kingdom lives
    and grows.
It echoes, endures, transforms the timidity of waves
And, knowledgeable of its grace and charm,
Gives purpose to the ocean roar and feeds,
Unsuspecting in the night, the lonely hunger of the stars.

FAITH AND THE GIFT

Somewhere in untraveled lands
A rock reflects its granite love
And from that rock the waters flow
To be ravaged by the desert sands.
    Consider the Rock.
This is neither the death of ice nor birth of grace:
It is the mystery of strength, new-found,
Feared and jeered by those who melt
For want of form and unearned peace.
Where night is thought a cancer of the light
There is no warmth.
    Consider the dark.
The chariot of the sun has long since burned
And ashes hold more promise than wanted dawn.
But Aurora was not so weak she could not blush--
And she prevails.
    Consider the dawn.
This is no journey for the strong, the great.
Only the gentle frail are worthy of the path.

Only the mute know the notes that echo
    from canyon walls
And only the brave need crossed staves
To point the way.
    Consider the path.
Amid the bitterness of silence, speak
To regain the Rock, the dark, the dawn, the path
Within the silence of your voice.
And in the deafness of your touch, heal the night.
There are no thanks in blind men's eyes
To barter for the gift of sight.
    Consider the gift.

FAITH AND FATE

The common heir to an uncommon fate
Breeds destiny in a triple bond:
Shared hands meet in a darkened cave,
Called life;
Shared oaths mingle in a written scroll,
Called life;
Shared goals stiffen in a transformed heart,
Called life.
And that threefold life lives on, beyond the when of time
Or the burden of space.
A spider weaves its web in the captive's doubts
And the eagle distains the hunter's pangs.
The suppleness of hope lies easy in the breast
For humanity itself is purer in this bond.
Renewed in renewing, dared in daring,
Symbolic in its symbols, but yet itself,
The bond and life grow on,
Terrible and beautiful in their peace.

FAITH AND DOUBT

Deep within the caverns of our doubt
There lurks an anxious shadow of our fears.
It lives its dance reflected on the cavern walls
And offers ashes respite from its blasting sun.
The wall, the dance, the ash are one in twilight sleep
While voices call, outside of sight or sound.
Yet here the coupled clasp, forsaking death,
Echoes down the promise always there.
Or other: the oyster feels its home in pain
And heals that pain with pearls.
Resplendent in its love, it weaves the gem
That shames a lesser hope, or greater fear.
The risk births pearls, too bright for sight or doubt.
The touch of peace, the shock of joy, surprise the heart
That pulses with the heart, not only yours or mine,
    but more.
The gift of sacrifice is warmly held to grow
Infolded in the all-consuming Rose of grace.

FAITH AND THE RAINBOW

Gored to beauty by misshaping winds,
The storm-rinsed dusk births rainbows
That hold Earth in place.
Horizons extend beyond pledged love
And coalesce to stars under the layered arch
And there grow brave.
Distilled by fire, the rainbow's gold flares forth
And lionizes into grace raw wounds.
The starving run to meet the dawn
And grasp new hope from trembling night.
A world at peace is bought on battlefields of pain
With lightening blasts and thunder fears.
Yet spilled blood means life, renewed in doubt.
Resplendent in its gold, the bow receives the homage
    of the light
And puts fresh strength in timid clouds
While lost raindrops find their way back home.

FAITH AND KNOWLEDGE

Once upon a time,
a long time ago in the only time that is really important,
a strong wind blew out of the North,
across the hills and mountains,
across the plains and the mesas,
across the seas and the valleys,
across the years and the ages,
and it came to rest and blow around a lonely hogan deep
within the rocks, sheltered by the cliffs.
Inside the hogan, First Woman groaned and panted,
she wailed and she trembled
and she gave birth to First Boy and First Girl,
both strong and healthy twins
with black hair and dark eyes,
with sharp ears and strong hands.
And First Woman said, "These are beautiful children,
too beautiful to stay in this lonely hogan,
deep within the rocks and sheltered by the cliffs."

37

So First Woman watched them grow and she planned
    for the day when she
would send them out of the lonely hogan
to go beyond the plains and the mesas,
beyond the seas and the valleys,
even beyond the years and the ages,

First Boy and First Girl grew stronger and more beautiful
    every day.
They played with Coyote and with Snake;
they slept with Bear and with Rabbit.
They learned to walk in the sun light and in the star light.
They learned how to swim in the waters and to walk
    on the frozen rivers.

And as they grew, First Boy looked at First Girl
    and he grew jealous.
She had longer hair and could run faste than he could.
She could weave baskets faster and better than he could.
She could grow corn bigger and tastier than he could.
So he grew jealous.

And as they grew, First Girl looked at First Boy
    and she grew jealous.
He could tame and ride a horse better than she could.
He could find fish in the waters faster and bigger
    than she could.
He could climb mountains faster and higher
    than she could.
So she grew jealous.

Both became restless and unhappy with their lives.

So First Girl and First Boy became angry with each other
and First Woman could see it was time for them to part.

And she said, "It is time for you, First Boy, to go your way
    to the West,
and it is time for you, First Girl, to go to the East.
And there you will find what you seek.
as Snake knows the sand
and Coyote knows the rocks.
And you will not know that you have found it
until you no longer seek it."

With that, First Woman gave to each child
    a magic leather sack.
Both sacks were the same and each contained
one eagle feather, caught in the light of a new moon,
one smooth stone, bleached white as snow
    by the noontime sun
and washed clean by the rains and the winds,
and three seeds from the lonely hogan,
which had been reaped and colored by laughter
    and tears.

The next morning, First Boy and First Girl left
    First Woman in her lonely hogan,
deep within the rocks and sheltered by the cliffs.
She watched as they strode largely out,
    First Boy to the West
and First Girl to the East.
And as she watched, she said to herself,
"Now it begins and I do not know how it will end
    although the ending is already here."

First Girl walked toward the morning star and she said,
"I know that I will never reach that star,
but I also know that it will be my guide."
She walked past the mesa with its gently blowing sands;
she walked beyond the hills with their gentle slopes;
she walked into the desert with its beckoning cactus;

she listened for Coyote to call her name gently
in the morning dew and the evening chill.
But Coyote remained silent.
Each morning she looked for her star
and she knew that she was answering an unknown voice
which urged her onward.

Now First Boy did not look back as he left his hogan.
He walked straight and tall into the West,
his shadow before him.
The darkness was not yet conquered by the light
but he knew he must find his own way without a star
and without a guide.
The hills in which he had played with First Girl were first
    beneath him, and then they were behind him.
He walked out of the mesas with their gently blowing
    sands;
he walked beyond the hills with their gentle slopes;
he walked into the desert with its beckoning cactus;
he listened for Coyote who did not call his name
in the morning dew and evening chill.
Each evening he watched the sun leave the earth
and travel to its rest beyond the mountains.
And each evening he marked his way for the morning
    journey.
He listened for the voice that would call his name
because he knew he could draw courage from that voice;
but the voice was silent
and so he walked into the silence and into the dark.

Now it happened that, one time when the sun grew weary,
a great darkness covered the land.
First Girl and First Boy had never seen such darkness
    that came in the middle of the day.
The sky was darker than night
but there were no stars to light the heavens.

The sky was darker than the depths of any cave
but there was no opening to show the way out.
The sky was so dark that neither knew which was the way
    up nor which was the way down.
The beauty of First Girl and the courage of First Boy
could not show them the paths
and could not call their names
and would not touch their faces.
Now the darkness grew even darker;
First Girl was no longer sure she was First Girl;
First Boy was no longer sure he was First Boy.
Though they were separated by miles and by ages,
they both found a shelter in the surrounding rocks.
They both pushed their way deep into the crevices of the
    rocks and waited.
The darkness began to withdraw slowly
slowly,
and, in time, the light returned so they could see
the rocks which protected them.
But they were completely lost when it was light enough
    again to travel.
First Girl looked toward the East
and First Boy looked toward the West
and they both saw scenes they had never seen before
and then they knew they were lost.

And then they both remembered that they had a magic
pouch
that First Woman had given them.
They each reached into the pouch
and took from it the feather of the eagle.
First Girl took the feather, held it into the waning darkness
and let the feather drift on the breeze.
The wind took the feather up, up,
and then drifted toward the morning star.

First Girl began then to follow after the feather until she
  could walk no more.
First Boy took out his feather, held it into the waning
  darkness and let the feather drift on the breeze.
The wind took the feather up, up,
and then drifted toward the promise of evening.
First Boy began then to follow the feather until he too could
  walk no more.

But since each one now had a direction to follow
they knew that the voice was calling them
and would never again be silent.

One day followed another,
one night came quietly after its twin,
and First Boy and First Girl traveled farther away from their
  hogan,
First Boy to the sunset and First Girl to the sunrise.
They depended on their Mother the Earth to provide
what they needed for their hunger,
and they depended on their Father the Sky to provide
the rains they needed for their thirst.
During the light time,
they walked as their hearts led them
through the heat of the blistering sun and
through the chill of the encroaching dusk.
Each day seemed the same
and yet each day was different
They walked carefully on the land, never harming or
  injuring the earth
upon which they set their footprints.
They met their old friends, Rabbit and Snake,
Coyote and Bear,
and they followed their paths through forests and deserts,
over rivers and valleys,
past hills and under arches.

But one day, their journey changed.
They each came to a huge cliff that rose from the ground like
    a giant monstrous huge and menacing.
They felt within themselves something like despair.
The cliff was so high they could not see the top,
nor could they see the birds fly above it.
They could not see ledges or protruding rocks
so they might climb.
Clouds came and surrounded them
so that they could no longer see even the cliff.
And though they could not see it,
they could feel it with their hands.
First Boy withdrew into himself and allowed his fear
to speak to his heart.
First Girl withdrew into herself and allowed her fear
to speak to her heart.

Each heard only silence,
but it was a deeper silence than the presence of no sound.
    But water washes rain;
desert sands blow with desert sands;
clouds move and talk to clouds;
and so too the rock in their magic pouches
would speak to the giant rock of the cliff.

They reached into their magic pouches and felt for
    the magic stone
First Woman had given them.
They each held the stone in their fingers,
then placed it in the palms of their hands.
They felt the smoothness and compared it to the roughness
    of the cliff;
they compared the even roundness of the stone
with the harsh edges of the cliff,
and they knew that now they could be safe
for they had rock of its rock,

substance of its substance,
hardness of its hardness,
strength of its strength.

What had stopped their journey would now be part of their
    journey;
what had made them fear now gave them great courage.
And they each knew that nothing outside of themselves
    could stop them.
Only what lurked deep in their hearts need ever cause them
    fear again.

First Boy and First Girl grew older and they grew wiser. But
    they did not grow happier.
They had used their magic feathers
and they had used their magic stones
but they also had a hollow in their hearts
which no direction and no courage could fill.
The waters from springs no longer tasted fresh and clear;
they no longer spoke to them of snow-capped mountains
nor of spring rains.
The waters from rivers no longer flowed in mystery and
    shadow,
no longer murmured gently of promises and protection.
The corn they ate no longer tasted of the richness of the
    field
nor gave off the sweet scent of sunrise.

In their sleep, they no longer saw visions of pastures and
    valleys; they no longer felt caressing breezes on their
    phantom selves.
Now they saw black pits and threatening hollows;
they felt fear and lostness, as though they belonged
    nowhere;
as though they had come from nowhere and were going
    nowhere.

And so they looked once more into their magic pouches
and found the three seeds that First Woman had given them.
They took each seed out very gently and examined each one
with infinite care.
First Girl took one seed and examined it closely.
The first seed reminded her of First Boy and the horses
    he tamed;
the second seed reminded her of the fish he caught with his
    bare hands;
and the third seed reminded her of the mountains he could
    climb with ease and speed.
Then she knew she must return to her hogan because the
    horse, the fish and the mountains
were calling her.
She threw the three seeds into the wind and followed the
    path they set.

At the same time, First Boy took out his three seeds
And examined the first one.
It reminded him of the corn that First Girl grew
    and he remembered how rich it tasted.
He took out the second seed and remembered the baskets
    she could weave
without effort and in such beauty.
He took out the third seed
and he remembered the color of First Girl's hair and the way
    it flowed in the wind as she raced over the mesa.
Then he knew that he must return to his hogan because the
    corn, the basket, and the hair were calling him.
He threw the three seeds into the wind
    and followed the path they set.

And so First Boy and First Girl began their return journeys,
First Girl to the West and First Boy to the East.
As they walked,

First Boy saw for the first time the light that comes over the
    mountains and beyond the plains.
He no longer saw his shadow as he walked into the night.
Now he felt the growing warmth of the sun as it began its
    march across the sky;
he felt the heat on his face after the night time chill
and he saw the desert flowers open to greet the newborn
    light.
His steps became swifter and more assured as he
    recognized his footprints in the drifting earth.

First Girl, as she walked into the West,
saw for the first time the death of the sun and its final gift of
    brilliant colors and shapes.
She felt the encroaching chill of the dark and the
    lengthening shadows that came after instead of in front of
    her.
She saw the flowers as they closed their arms around
    themselves and prepared for the period of sleep and
    ingathering strength.
She saw the sun leave behind him the little lights that
    marked his passage
and they reminded her of her star before the sun embraced
    all the lesser lights
and gave warmth to her world of wandering.
Her steps became swifter and more assured as she
    recognized her footprints in the drifting earth.

Although they knew and did not know it,
First Boy and First Girl were nearing each other across
    many dangers and adventures.
All they knew was the hollows in their hearts were both
    growing and diminishing;
they were burning and chilling at the same time;
they were impelling and restful at the same time;
they were demanding and comforting at the same time.

They did not think about the mystery in their hearts
and they did not slow their footsteps.
In the hollows of their hearts
they heard the voice of First Woman who had said, "You
must go," but now the voice said, "You must come."
Hers was the last sound they heard as they laid down to
sleep
and it was the first sound they heard as they opened their
eyes in the morning.
The voice became stronger the closer they came to their
hogan.
It was as though the land itself spoke,
and the sun spoke
and the stars spoke.

At last they heard above the sound of First Woman's voice
another voice.
It was soft and gentle and could easily have been missed
If they had listened too intently to their own footsteps.
The new sound brought them to the river they had each
crossed,
First Boy to the West and First Girl to the East.
Their journeys had made them very hot and dry
and they thought they could travel no farther.
When they looked down, they saw the water
that had called them
and they saw that the water was clear and cool,
but deep within the clearness there was a greater clarity
which could only be called mystery.

They both knelt down to drink;
they plunged their faces into the rushing water
and the water now refreshed them and the coolness
comforted them.
New life then flowed through their bodies
and the hollows in their hearts began to fill.

47

When First Girl looked into the river she saw, not her face,
but the face of First Boy.
When First Boy looked into the river he saw, not his face,
but the face of First Girl.

They looked across the river at each other;
they smiled as they saw themselves in each other as their
    reflections became one.
"Now," said First Girl, "now we can return to First Woman
    and to our own hogan."
"Yes, now," said First Boy, "we can return to First Woman
    and, then,
we can begin can search for First Man."
"Indeed," said First Girl, "but I think we have already
    found him."

Considerations for the Story

First Part:
first beginnings
the journey of life,
letting go and being sent out
unity which is undifferentiated is just sameness
each one has an amulet or token of strength, comfort,
    security
journey is always anticipated, even after it has begun
east is place of sun rise, Venus as morning star,
west is place of sunset, death, courage, averting star which is
    also Venus.

Second Part:
each person needs faith in something faith is risky and
    fragile faith never arises until we need it
and cannot he dictated or commanded
we are lost because no one knows his/her name=identity
feather blows softly but reveals great strength (eagle) one
    must have faith in something.

Third Part:
all face obstacles that seem insurmountable
the obstacle and its suppression are the same thing
we need hope which is the same as despair with, instead of
    without, courage
faith gives them a reason to hope
courage over fear.

Fourth Part:
faith and hope are not enough without love
we love only those things that we know
we treasure the small things more than the great.

Fifth Part:
unity of the male and female for wholeness in each
they know themselves only in recognizing another
waters of baptism which is a new way of life
as with all journeys, we have what we seek
we always need to be on a journey and are never done
we know where we are only after we have left -life as
    homecoming.

Entire story is that God is the beginning, the companion and
    the end of each life's journey. We do not seek him but
    realize that he is always with us. But we must seek him
    to understand ourselves and find our wholeness.

FAITH AND HOPE

Gored to beauty by misshaping winds,
The storm-rinsed dusk births rainbows
That hold Earth in place.
Horizons extend beyond pledged love
And coalesce to stars under the layered arch
And there grow brave.
Distilled by fire, the rainbow's gold flares forth
And lionizes into grace raw wounds.
The starving run to meet the dawn
And grasp new hope from trembling night.
A world at peace is bought on battlefields of pain
With lightening blasts and thunder fears.
Yet spilled blood means life, renewed in doubt.
Resplendent in its gold, the bow receives the homage
    of the light
And puts fresh strength in timid clouds
While lost raindrops find their way back home.

FAITH AND THE PEACOCK

Before the peacock knew the pangs of pride
Or the eagle felt the thirst for flight,
Once upon that time, so many times ago,
In the only time that is ever real,
The sun grew jealous of his might
And sent the stars to carry brilliant messages of peace.
Into the darkened corridors of doubt
Where even deserts feared to grow, they flashed.
The fog in garden fens whorled about,
Transformed into imaged images of love.
And the depths found voice to call the depths
While stars and shadows danced.
Within that dance the meaning found its sight
And love-quested leaves became themselves
In union with the mountain streams.
The journey of the star, the leaf,
The light, the stream
Became one uninterrupted song of praise.
Forever became a crippled clown;

The when of hope and the then of dreams
Gave way--strange gift--to the now of life.
And the sun rejoiced in the cacophony of joy
And lent one particular leaf the seed
That burst apart in ecstasies of self.
The green of hope, the grey of death,
The red of quest, the blue of peace
All rushed forth and rainbows, new-hatched, blushed.
Now all who saw the star became the star,
    And the star grew brighter.
All who loved the leaf became the leaf,
    And the leaf thrilled.
All who risked the stream became the stream,
    And the stream rushed forth.
And all who bathed in light became the light,
    And the light laughed the dawn to birth.

REQUIEM FOR A DREAM

Hardwon among the struggles fought in doubt
A distant dream, like a hand-sized cloud, takes shape
In the unseen horizons of the mind.
And in that cloud-dream there are undreamed kingdoms,
Places of light and peace,
Of grace and greatness,
Which repel by their attraction.
Hidden storms crouch, expectant and humorless,
Drenching the fog-filled fact,
Their deluge more than earth or thought can bear.
A sort of calm takes root and mocks the dream,
Betrays the dreamer,
In formulation of the less than real.
Is the storm less fierce for being spent,
The cost more dear for being past?
And yet the shapeless cloud lives on,
A memory that missed existence in the accident of time.
And is there not form in the formless,
Shape in the shapeless,
Danger in the untried?
Even hollows have their depths,
Shadows their mysteries.
For what is the death of a dream
But a vision's birth?

LONELINESS

The isolated oneness that divides and not unites
I dread.
The opulent pain of unshared shadows
I fear.
That Half that molders in unhatched graves
I reject.
The forgotten feel of blistered flesh
I crave.
The touched may call attention, care, and charm.
But do towers live for passing clouds
Or mountains for a smothering snow?
The leaf, a part of huge kingdoms, dies,
One more death among the millions dead.
Was it any less a leaf, its bloom the less for more?
I cannot find the light.
The feel of it tells me right is south in the winter play.
But sunset calls louder than a daemon lover
Over plucked bones and bleached skulls.

For all the voices of Cocytus mingle
   in the fevered thought
And suck the unsaid promise from lying lips
   and empty arms.

DEATH: A CONSIDERATION

Outraged by life, ungentled by death,
We greet the sacred mound and call it ours.
The recognition swarms the brain
And violates the heart.
It wrenches sinew from bone
And sucks blood from constricting veins
To find a haven in uneasy sleep.

We peer from submissive heads to ambivilate
   the chosen stance
And rage.
It is not the star of this dark hour
That guides our hopes,
But some dank cave with fetid waves
Which impels our minds, cripples our dreams.

The serpent's lesser self holds sway,
Singing of his victory.
But its voice is drowned and doomed
In the undulating swell of children's song,
Their melody untested by howling winds,
But assured and clear.
For their notes gain strength in the empty tomb
And their grave air hollows out for us
An outrage for a home.

CHRIST IN THE DESERT

With scorpions and sands my only friends
These days have dragged beyond numbness and doubt.
The grit of dust tastes fresh in this constant wind
From rainless clouds.
I see lies in shadows of these stones
And my constricted bowels crave rocks for bread.
The texture of the wheat more rich than honeycomb;
The dew from rocks more sweet than Alexander's ocean
    spread.
My hunger feeds upon itself and gnaws my guts
With whispers from decaying texts.
By what miracle of sight do my senses howl for rest
From this noontime heat?
The heavy air shimmers in undulating waves of sun,
For what should be is not.
That distant plain shows cities
Full in grain and praise and people noise.
There would be no more to think or do,

But all is done in one quick kiss with ease.
My arms feel full, empty of a scepter's weight;
My head is light without confining crowns.
Why barter freedom for empty cheers and angel wings?
The phantoms cease and, in their place,
A universe of light-specked, brain-burned stars holds,
Anticipating destiny's reverse and trumpeted majesty,
Mine for merest touch beyond mere desire.
A scorpion stops at my footprint mark and waits.
It tests the depth the heel has made in sand,
It's arched tail flickers, prepares for bravery beyond its size,
Then plunges down, no thought of other routes.
I would not, for stone or plain or light,
Deny its quest.
If that for less, how much for more?
I will not bid the sun take back its heat,
The rock undo its strength,
A star holds back its light.
It well may be I will know another thirst,
Blister in the merciless noon of another day.
But I am content in my hunger,
Replete in my unfed desires.
But, ah! the temple bells blow free
As the restless scorpion moves on to its shifting home.

THE MAGI

They called us wise because they thought us not
And derided the purpose of our dream.
Their laughter was not less strong than their contempt
At our thirst for stars.
Not stars, but star that would not fit the winter night.
The Sisters Seven warned us by no show of rain
And pale Merope brightened, now proud of her trade with
    men.
These signs we read and did not understand.
We offered three young bulls to Urania
And a fatted calf to Marduk.
Sacrificial smoke shrouded the new born star,
Its heat burned our restless hearts with longing
And our aged bones with flight.
And so we came.
We were all too old for extended search or desert tents,
For questions that mocked and cutting snears.

But we followed the ache and the ghastly light
And came at last to our journey's end.
I cannot speak for my companions,
Exhausted by puzzles and alien tongues.
I can say only that the sky knew of our approach
And the star of our quest.
I do not remember the long trek home,
Or the welcome,
Or the effect.
I know the restlessness has not ceased within my breast,
Nor have my eyes yet dried from uneasy tears.
We have seen too much to speak,
And the only sound I now can hear is an infant's wail
Above the howling winds.

OBITUARY

Twenty-five lines in a throwaway text
Do not sing in hearts full of memories.
There should be rage and belief and the belief in love,
Not outmoded, forgotten dates in dusty catalogues.
Blood on lintels should forewarn the passer-by
Of burning passion within,
Of smothered pride.
Where is the anger at the thrice-read letter of rejection?
The tears on the once-sent letter of praise?
Where is the apology for the days on days
With never a zenithed noon?
Where is the dream, undeterred by defeat,
Or the stillborn vision, waiting to be shared?
The clawed hours of superstition repelled,
Or the darker nights of doubt-tossed sleep?
Where is the loss of Anthony's strength
Turned into victorious struggle?
How have twenty-five lines sketched all that was,
All that might have been,

A life?
Twenty-five lines, and a name in caps,
Do not sing in hearts full of memories

PROPHETS

Beware old men in temples,
Eyes wild, brow fevered, speech prophetic,
Who see beyond the past to purpose.
They will not give you comfort in sleep or rest in days.
They mouth riddles they cannot solve;
They see horizons they cannot reach;
They hear voices that do not speak.
Beware their fire and their ice,
Their dream too old to die, too young to live.
Beware their message which demands too little
and leaves too much.
They do not lie; therefore they are dangerous.
The spell they cast makes magic of dross, opals of tears.

Expect to stand at the abyss's edge if you would listen
	To their cant
And see a vulture in a sparrow's flight.
Prepare for battle with a child's toy
And dam the ocean with a broken stump.
The choice they give is narrow and their reward unsure.
And yet,
And yet, for all the violence they initiate,
They show the only way to peace.

FAITH AND THE SANDS

The crippling sands lie empty in their promise.
Golden in their light, they suck the life from stars
And shift their messages into patterned rills.
Derisive sounds they make against a never-winter wind.
But settled in their dunes, the vast enigma grows
And brazens out the lies, and waits.
It waits for birth--its own--from the blistered sun
To die reborn and beautiful.
The grace within the shell bursts forth
And its nucleus of splintered dreams weeps joy.
Juxtaposed against its nightless moon and dayless skies
Its vastness beats a throb of hope.
It thrills the blood in bloodless veins and bleaches leprous
	bones.
Enigma still, enigmatic to itself, it shames the sands with
	truth.
Ten thousand thousand cries of peace, released amid the
	crystal cries, Revive and live.
And each felt grain becomes itself,
	Golden in its light;
		Golden in its love.

TRIPTYCH

Only winds guard the ancient ceremony of decay.
Toneless voices whisper in the long-dead urgency that hope
    is near.
Protected by the waning moon, the fertile rite takes power,
Making fertile the undreamed wish.
Behind crumpled portals, the ghosts still watch for
    vengeance,
And weep.
Frustrated in the night, the echo of the warrior's cry
    commingles
With the victim's wail;
Battled inches scream in pain and treachery
While whisked arrows clash, spent and ineffectual.
The foes embrace in death-locked pose, unresolved by
    strength,
And death itself is wounded by the strife.
Time may heal or fester broken faith;
Great spirits hide in shame from suppliants' hands.
They leave only the healing winds, guardians of oblivion,
To salve the loss,
And clutched tucked rock pays tribute to inevitable defeat.

II

The last Ancient of Days stood silent
    on his wind-swept height.
Alone, he surveyed the ancestral patrimony,
    laid waste by waste;
Alone, he spoke the long-dead tongue that
    brought rain to fields,
    and heat from the sun;
Alone, he shivered at lost magic and forgotten rites;
He alone.
Smoke of spent yesterdays stung his eyes,

Left rills of too-easy tears on his earthen face.
The thought of one or many years was gone;
All past moons were one.
No blinding point of glory, no glaring shame of regret,
Vied in his mind for value or for second life.
No longer could he stir at stallion's charge
Or laugh at arrows, bent by game.
His time for return and fetal death had come.
The moon had lighted this same scene in other times,
    the old times, the gone times.
Other eyes had shared the sight.
Other faces had felt the harvest wind
And other hands had plucked the ready corn.
Dancing feet had pushed their weight against the earth,
    apologetic for the unintended pain.

The rhythm of the sun and growth kept faith
With the rhythm of the moon and birth.
It was not good or bad, advantage or loss;
It was the gift.

The circling stars, full of their importance and design,
Gave way to fields, full of sunrise and waiting grain.
The women, full of unborn warriors, held promise of
    completed peace.
But then the magic moved to other lands
And the fullness shrank before a stronger charm.
The risk of repeating timeless rituals was run
And danger threatened every pleading rite.
The navel of the earth had moved;
Grace settled with the cooling sun.
No clouds spun patterns on the mountain's rim;
The benefice of heaven fled to more favored sons.
The river wept its last few tears and,
With the ritual way of life and death,
Passed beyond the call of dance or prayer.